ELISHA COOPER

Ice Cream

Greenwillow Books
An Imprint of HarperCollins*Publishers*

It starts with a cow.

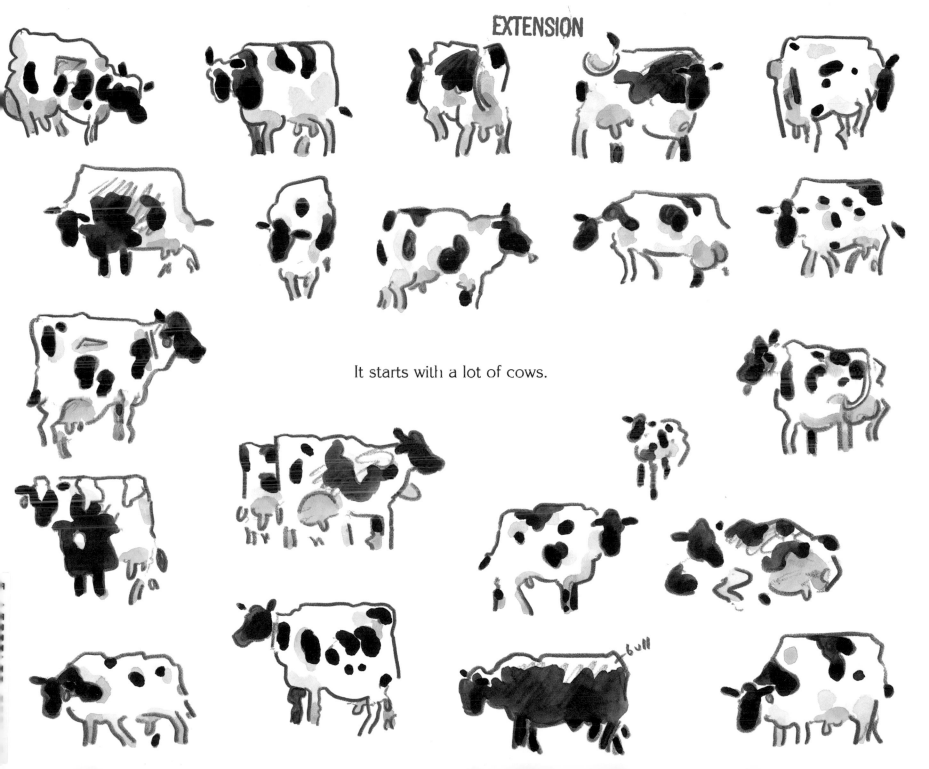

It starts with a lot of cows.

It also starts with a grass field and the sun above and a nearby body of water and all the hay,

grass

peer

grain, and rain that feeds the cows and fills their udders with milk. What is it? It's ice cream.

Every day the cows graze in their field until it's time for milking. The cows have big, curious eyes, swishing tails, and bony hips. Each wears a tag in one ear.

Mud and brambles mat the hair on their stomachs. When they walk to the milking barn, their udders swing from side to side.

The cows enter the milking barn in groups. Their udders are swollen, and warm to the touch. Milk comes out steaming.

The farmer squirts each teat by hand, then attaches four suction teat cups, which connect to the milking machine.

Each cow gives about five gallons of milk.

When the udder is empty, the farmer
removes the cups and dabs disinfectant on
each teat. The farmer says, *"Move! Cows!"*
hoses the floor, repeats the process.

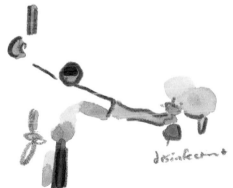

Everything gets wet. The farmer
wears an apron and rubber boots.

The cows eat grain while they're being milked. They chew in
a circular motion with their noses in the air. They're messy—
corn and pellets and cotton seed cover the concrete floor.

A row of cows. A milking barn full of low sounds: the *FUMP, FUMP* of the suction cups; the *CHUG, CHUG, CHUG* of milk spurting through plastic tubes; the *WHISH* of suction released; the rustle of birds' wings swooping through the rafters; the rumble of chewing. The milk travels from the tubes to a pipe, then disappears through a hole in the wall.

EXTENSION

The milk in the pipe shoots into a steel tank in the milk house. The tank hums and keeps the milk cool. In the evening the milk truck arrives.

With a long dipper the milk truck man takes a sample that will be tested to make sure the milk is safe to use.

With a hose he pumps milk to his truck. When the tank is empty, he opens the milk house door, and three cats

rush in to lap up spilled milk. They have white whiskers and look happy until the farm dog chases them off.

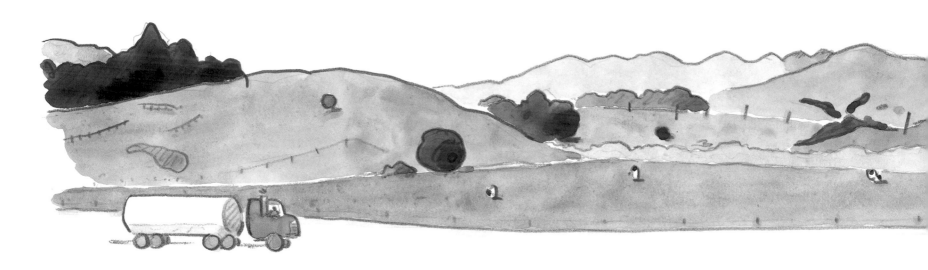

The truck drives through the country, stopping at other farms until its belly is full of six thousand gallons of milk. It crawls along one-lane roads,

downshifts up among hills, winds down through a forest,
then enters a highway, crosses a bridge, and reaches the city.

The milk truck pulls up to the milk co-op. Milk goes through pipes into storage tanks, through a separator that parts the milk from the cream, throu

a machine where some of the milk is condensed, then back through pipes to separate trucks. The milk goes through a lot.

Trucks carry cream and milk and condensed milk across town to the ice cream factory. The ice cream factory is plain and square, with silos waiting on one side and a sweet smell coming through open windows.

As the trucks pump their milk and cream into the silos, a worker records the amounts. The silos are so big, the worker could swim laps across them.

Other trucks arrive at the ice cream factory. They unload sugar,

fudge, cocoa, malt, vanilla extract, chocolate chips, berries, fruit,

candy, pecans, pistachios, mangoes, egg yolks, marshmallows,

corn syrup, emulsifiers, peanut butter, cookie dough, brownies.

The ingredients come packed in paper bags and cardboard boxes

and plastic jugs, and stack within an inch of the ceiling.

On the top floor of the ice cream factory is a small laboratory. A bench in the center is covered with bowls, beakers, blenders, small freezers. Scientists in white coats hover over the bench. They create ice cream recipes.

They stir ingredients teaspoon by teaspoon—tasting, adding, tasting—and decide to add more chocolate, or a lot more chocolate. One scientist wipes her hands on her coat when she finds the perfect formula.

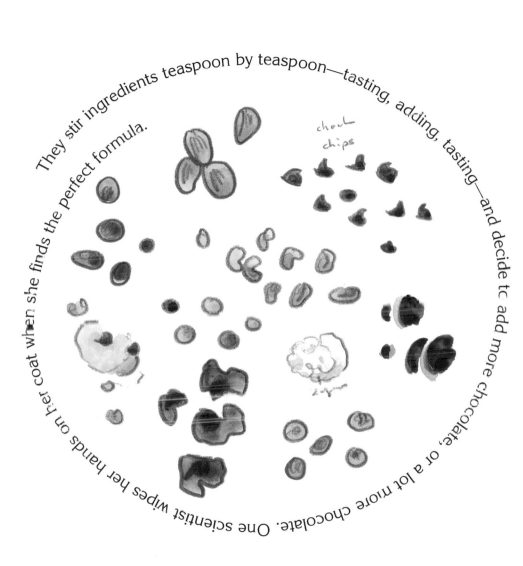

choc chips

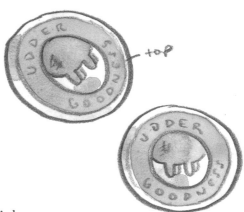

The ice cream factory orders its own special cartons. A name and a drawing and the factory logo are printed on lids and flat pieces of cardboard. A machine rounds the flats into pint containers, gallon containers, and three-gallon containers.

Cartons take shape. On the back of the cartons is a list of the ingredients that will soon be inside.

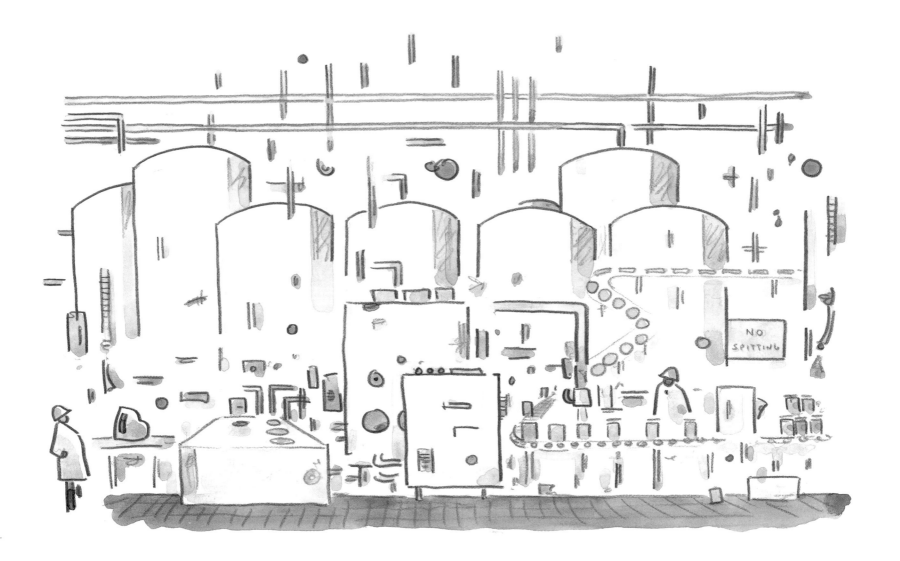

The ice cream machine sits on the factory floor. It is a steel, piston-pumping, cream-dripping, gadget-whirring, water-spraying, pipe-rattling, chocolate-leaking animal. A sign on the wall says, "No Spitting." Drains dot the floor. Workers wearing aprons, hard hats, hair nets, and beard nets take care of the machine.

Workers program the recipe into a computer. The computer tells the ice cream machine what to do. Cream and milk and condensed milk churn together with sugars in the mixing tanks,

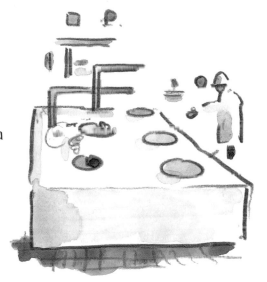

then are pasteurized and homogenized, then join vanilla or chocolate or another flavor in the flavor vat,

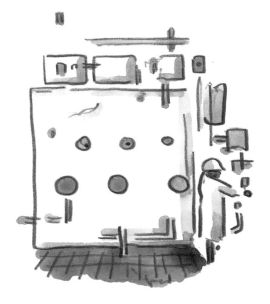

then travel to the freezer, where paddles whip the mixture gently into ice cream.

In the hopper the ice cream mixes with cookie dough or brownies or berries,

which workers feed into the machine,

then shoots down the filler tube and—

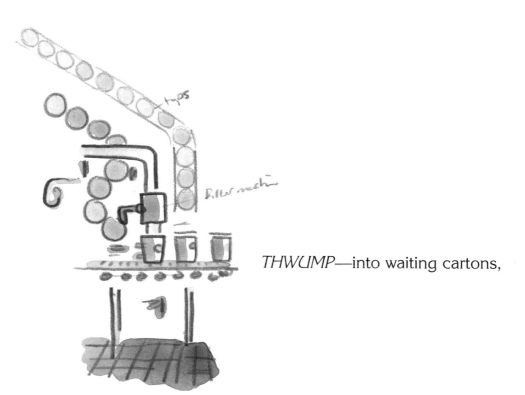

THWUMP—into waiting cartons,

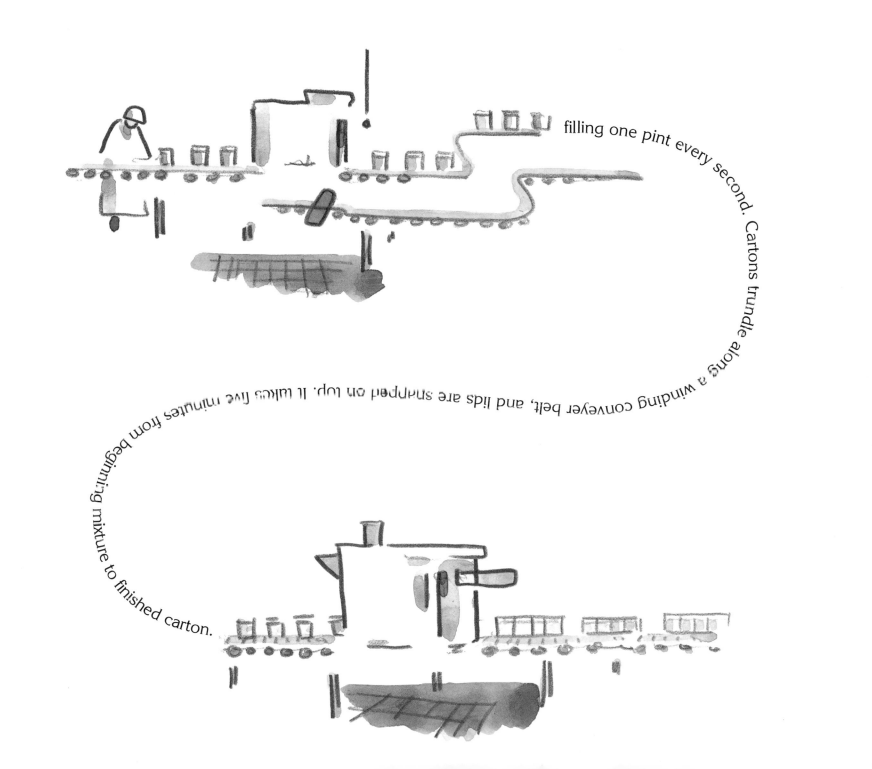

filling one pint every second. Cartons trundle along a winding conveyer belt, and lids are snapped on top. It takes five minutes from beginning mixture to finished carton.

The taster removes a carton from the conveyer belt

 and cuts it in half with a double-handled knife.

 She checks for quality: look, smell, texture, taste.

 She tastes with a gold spoon, which leaves no aftertaste.

 Her cheeks bulge as she swirls ice cream around her palate.

 She smacks her lips, says, "*Marvelous!*"

 then rinses. The taster is so important to the ice cream factory

that it insures her tongue.

The conveyer belt carries boxes of cartons through the try-tray room where the temperature is forty degrees below zero.

Cold hardens the ice cream. As the conveyer belt enters the warehouse, a forklift lifts the cartons, carries them to a machine that wraps them in plastic,

then stacks them high on wooden pallets.

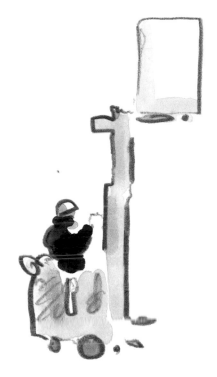

The forklift driver wears a woolen hat with a hole for his eyes.

Other workers wear puffy jackets.

At the ice cream factory, workers load boxes of cartons into refrigerated ice cream trucks. A driver checks his clipboard to make sure he has all the ice cream he needs. Then he drives to grocery stores and stocks their iceboxes,

to supermarkets and fills their freezers, and to corner ice cream parlors,
where the three-gallon tubs he delivers will be scooped into cones.

The ice cream truck has one last delivery. It leaves the city and crosses the bridge, enters a highway, downshifts up through a forest,

winds down among round hills, crawls along one-lane
roads, and drives through the country to the farm.

The ice cream truck pulls up to the milking barn. The driver gets out and gives a few cartons to the farmer.

The farmer thanks him, then walks out to the field and eats ice cream with his cows. Well, he lets them watch.

GLOSSARY

Condensed Milk: A form of milk that results from heating whole milk so that water is lost to evaporation and the volume is reduced by half.

Co-op: A cooperative organization of farmers created to share the costs of buying and using the expensive machinery needed to process milk.

Emulsifier: After milk is homogenized, a substance is added to it that wraps around any small bits of fat that are still present and prevents them from lumping back together, keeping the milk smooth.

Homogenization: Fresh milk, which contains particles of fat, is forced through tiny holes in a machine that breaks down the particles and makes the milk smooth and even.

Hopper: A bin with slanted sides attached by a tube to a container below. Ingredients are put into the hopper, and gravity causes them to fall through the tube into the material in the container, where they are mixed together.

Palate: The roof of the mouth, where food can be held while the tongue tastes it.

Pasteurization: A heating process that destroys enough bacteria in fresh milk so that it does not spoil quickly. This lengthens the period of time in which milk can be refrigerated, stored, and used safely.

Udder: The sack that hangs under a cow's belly, where the milk produced by the cow is stored. Through teats, or nipples, milk is drawn by the cow's calves or by the farmer's milking machine.

For the cows of Point Reyes

Ice Cream. Copyright © 2002 by Elisha Cooper. All rights reserved. Printed in Singapore by Tien Wah Press. www.harperchildrens.com
Watercolors and pencil were used to prepare the full-color art. The text type is Korinna.

Library of Congress Cataloging-in-Publication Data: Cooper, Elisha. Ice cream / by Elisha Cooper. p. cm. "Greenwillow Books." Summary: A step-by-step exploration of how ice cream is made, beginning with the healthy foods cows eat to produce good milk, and ending with a carton of frozen treat. ISBN 0-06-001423-7 (trade). ISBN 0-06 001424-5 (lib. bdg.) 1. Ice cream, ices, etc.—Juvenile literature. 2. Ice cream industry—Juvenile literature. [1. Ice cream, ices, etc. 2. Ice cream industry.] I. Title. TX795 C66 2002 637'.4—dc21 2001040495
10 9 8 7 6 5 4 3 2   First Edition